# PAGES
## TORN
### FROM A PLAGUE...

STEVEN M. WUEBKER

**BALBOA**.PRESS

A DIVISION OF HAY HOUSE

Balboa Press books may be ordered through booksellers or by contacting:

Balboa Press
A Division of Hay House
1663 Liberty Drive
Bloomington, IN 47403
www.balboapress.com
844-682-1282

Because of the dynamic nature of the Internet, any web addresses or links contained in this book may have changed since publication and may no longer be valid. The views expressed in this work are solely those of the author and do not necessarily reflect the views of the publisher, and the publisher hereby disclaims any responsibility for them.

The author of this book does not dispense medical advice or prescribe the use of any technique as a form of treatment for physical, emotional, or medical problems without the advice of a physician, either directly or indirectly. The intent of the author is only to offer information of a general nature to help you in your quest for emotional and spiritual well-being. In the event you use any of the information in this book for yourself, which is your constitutional right, the author and the publisher assume no responsibility for your actions.

Any people depicted in stock imagery provided by Getty Images are models, and such images are being used for illustrative purposes only. Certain stock imagery © Getty Images.

Print information available on the last page.

ISBN: 979-8-7652-3327-6 (sc)
ISBN: 979-8-7652-3329-0 (hc)
ISBN: 979-8-7652-3328-3 (e)

Library of Congress Control Number: 2022915312

Balboa Press rev. date: 10/14/2022

# Dedication

*To my husband Joel...*
*for always encouraging me to follow my dreams with passion,*
*and to be passionate about my dreams.*
*This is for you, my love.*

# Contents

Preface - - - - - - - - - - - - - - - - - - - - - - - - - - - - - - - - - - - - - - - - xiii
"Composium" - - - - - - - - - - - - - - - - - - - - - - - - - - - - - - - - - - - - -xv

"The Skeletal Remains of Trees" - - - - - - - - - - - - - - - - - - - - - - - 1
"Ode to the Ironies of Spring" - - - - - - - - - - - - - - - - - - - - - - - 5
"Plague" - - - - - - - - - - - - - - - - - - - - - - - - - - - - - - - - - - - - - - - 7
"Self-reflections in rain puddles" - - - - - - - - - - - - - - - - - - - - - 9
"The Attractions of a Wayfaring Soul Traveler" - - - - - - - - - - - -11
"Fog on the fields, reminiscent...hazily" - - - - - - - - - - - - - - - 13
"Ascension, be careful what you wish for..." - - - - - - - - - - - - - 15
"The Deafening of Silence" - - - - - - - - - - - - - - - - - - - - - - - - - 17
"Ouroboros-ian Commutes" - - - - - - - - - - - - - - - - - - - - - - - - 19
"Book Store" - - - - - - - - - - - - - - - - - - - - - - - - - - - - - - - - - - 21
"Winter, darkest..." - - - - - - - - - - - - - - - - - - - - - - - - - - - - - - 23
"Beach House Blinds (shadow-grates)" - - - - - - - - - - - - - - - - 25
"Concentric Ripples" - - - - - - - - - - - - - - - - - - - - - - - - - - - - - 29
"Life in a candle jar" - - - - - - - - - - - - - - - - - - - - - - - - - - - - - 31
"Full moonlight through the trees, high" - - - - - - - - - - - - - - - - 33
"The Regimentation of a Pine Forest" - - - - - - - - - - - - - - - - - 35
"Dawakening" - - - - - - - - - - - - - - - - - - - - - - - - - - - - - - - - - 37
"Mornings at the lake" - - - - - - - - - - - - - - - - - - - - - - - - - - - - 39
"Another Round" - - - - - - - - - - - - - - - - - - - - - - - - - - - - - - - - 41
"Channeling my inner teenager self – 1970s" - - - - - - - - - - - - 45
"Prometheus the Forethinker rides solo again." - - - - - - - - - - - 47
"Skating on a thin putting green" - - - - - - - - - - - - - - - - - - - - - 49
"Ahhhhhhhhhnother Holiday Party" - - - - - - - - - - - - - - - - - - 51
"Mr. Straw, vespillō" - - - - - - - - - - - - - - - - - - - - - - - - - - - - - 53
"Tele-evangeli-vision" - - - - - - - - - - - - - - - - - - - - - - - - - - - - 57
Remembering...while packing for a long trip." - - - - - - - - - - - - 61
"Awaiting Spring, too early" - - - - - - - - - - - - - - - - - - - - - - - - 63
"Projects: Memory Drive" - - - - - - - - - - - - - - - - - - - - - - - - - - 65
"Waiting to burn" - - - - - - - - - - - - - - - - - - - - - - - - - - - - - - - 67
"What if...?" - - - - - - - - - - - - - - - - - - - - - - - - - - - - - - - - - - 69
"The Blue Beacon of Hope" - - - - - - - - - - - - - - - - - - - - - - - - 71

"An afternoon cantering gait taken beside a cornfield on a summer day" - - - - - - - - - - - - - - - - - - - - - - - - - - - - - - - 75
"Art, 2" - - - - - - - - - - - - - - - - - - - - - - - - - - - - - - - - - - - - - - - 77
"Winter again.....again." - - - - - - - - - - - - - - - - - - - - - - - - - - - 79
"The last 20 minutes on the train into L'Enfant Plaza, Washington DC" - - - - - - - - - - - - - - - - - - - - - - - - - - - - - 81
"a place you'd never tell anyone you've ever been..." - - - - - - - - 83
"Hard Dusk" - - - - - - - - - - - - - - - - - - - - - - - - - - - - - - - - - - - - 85
"Early storms" - - - - - - - - - - - - - - - - - - - - - - - - - - - - - - - - - - 87
"Dark Matters (from whence)" - - - - - - - - - - - - - - - - - - - - - - - 89
"Early Morning" - - - - - - - - - - - - - - - - - - - - - - - - - - - - - - - - - 91
"Opposite of Time" - - - - - - - - - - - - - - - - - - - - - - - - - - - - - - - 93
"Winds of Tar" - - - - - - - - - - - - - - - - - - - - - - - - - - - - - - - - - - 95
"Il Pagliaccio Della Morté (the clown of death)" - - - - - - - - - - - 99
"tres hermanas" - - - - - - - - - - - - - - - - - - - - - - - - - - - - - - - - -103
"And people wonder why religion as a second language is so hard to learn..." - - - - - - - - - - - - - - - - - - - - - - - - - - - - 105
"Inflation and a Winter War" - - - - - - - - - - - - - - - - - - - - - - - -107
"The carnival barker in winter" - - - - - - - - - - - - - - - - - - - - - - 109
"An exasperated mess in Suburban, America" - - - - - - - - - - - -111
"Winter, never ending" - - - - - - - - - - - - - - - - - - - - - - - - - - - 113
"Untitled" - - - - - - - - - - - - - - - - - - - - - - - - - - - - - - - - - - - - -115
"Abstractions and Memories" - - - - - - - - - - - - - - - - - - - - - - -119
"When Ego met God" - - - - - - - - - - - - - - - - - - - - - - - - - - - - -121
"The Currencies of Being" - - - - - - - - - - - - - - - - - - - - - - - - - -123
"The intertwined bands of the universe" - - - - - - - - - - - - - - -125
"Climbing icicles and chasing snowbows" - - - - - - - - - - - - - -127
"a mild case of the ceruleans" - - - - - - - - - - - - - - - - - - - - - -131
"Untitled" - - - - - - - - - - - - - - - - - - - - - - - - - - - - - - - - - - - - -133
"On middle-aging" - - - - - - - - - - - - - - - - - - - - - - - - - - - - - - -139
"Reincarnating revenge, recycling hate" - - - - - - - - - - - - - - -141
"Slow Down" - - - - - - - - - - - - - - - - - - - - - - - - - - - - - - - - - - -143
"Landing at night, Columbus, 3am" - - - - - - - - - - - - - - - - - -145
"The lion, the lamb, and the snake" - - - - - - - - - - - - - - - - - -147
"Aurora Borealis, credentis" - - - - - - - - - - - - - - - - - - - - - - - -149
"Harp-n-Crie" - - - - - - - - - - - - - - - - - - - - - - - - - - - - - - - - - -151
"Brain zaps; the anti-depressant alarm" - - - - - - - - - - - - - - -153
"The Girl on Top of the World" - - - - - - - - - - - - - - - - - - - - - -155
"Lonely" - - - - - - - - - - - - - - - - - - - - - - - - - - - - - - - - - - - - - -159
"A valley in a field in springtime" - - - - - - - - - - - - - - - - - - - -163
"In the court of pillars" - - - - - - - - - - - - - - - - - - - - - - - - - - - -167

"Sponge" - - - - - - - - - - - - - - - - - - - - - - - - - - - - - - - - - - - - - - -171
"Cedar" (for my father) - - - - - - - - - - - - - - - - - - - - - - - - - - - - -173
"Pondering Moons" - - - - - - - - - - - - - - - - - - - - - - - - - - - - - - - - -175
"Newsprint Poetry" - - - - - - - - - - - - - - - - - - - - - - - - - - - - - - - - -177
"While reincarnating memories..." - - - - - - - - - - - - - - - - - - - - -179

Postscript - - - - - - - - - - - - - - - - - - - - - - - - - - - - - - - - - - - - - - -181
Photo Credits - - - - - - - - - - - - - - - - - - - - - - - - - - - - - - - - - - - - -183
Acknowledgements and Gratitude - - - - - - - - - - - - - - - - - - - - -185

# Preface

*These pages came about from a period of lockdown, of quarantine, from a "time-space" when one was not always allowed to go outside, but one was always able to look within...*

*Universal memes of "monk, chunk, hunk, or drunk" abounded across the Internet during the pandemic days, predicting human outcomes from a period of isolation.*

*I chose "thunk" as an alternative option.*

*These selections are from within...intentionally not dated, a chronologically-twisted rollercoaster some researcher, somewhere, may someday decide to ride.*

*And just like that well-ridden coaster, the lack of dates detract nothing from the ominously slow progression of uphill exhilaration through the downward spirals of lost hope during the recent global pandemic.*

*At the end of all the days, they are just words on pages...*

## "Composium"

Definition: a mentally composed symposium.

(Noun, probably)

- used in times when large gatherings were not.
- could be a verb, maybe - "composium-ing".

"You'll have that at this time of year..." – said someone.

Walking in the forest
shedding my deciduous memories
      of you
      of long ago
once again...

Moving onward, moving upward
just as nature's spires
surrounding me do;
I am no longer...

Roots holding me steadfast and
lichen slowly mocking my decay,
sunlight reminding me
that leaves continue to fall away
but my memories of you never will.

And I walk on...


**"The Skeletal Remains of Trees"**

**"Pusha of Elk Mountain"**
**Photo: David Hellard**

**Inspiration for "The Skeletal Remains of Trees"**

Birds chirping
daffodils blooming
trees awakening
clouds slowly rumbling
away to their distance,
      the songs of Mother Nature are echoing
      among the silent morning background
ahh...the ironies of spring...

Shelter in place
among Mother Nature's majesty
in your place that is shelter.
The world
everyone's oyster, yet stuck within shells
seeking to find a lost
pearl within...
seeking spring
to begin again...

So burst the window forth
enjoy this day Mother Nature
hath made...
the rains have come
and will come again
but today
today
today is another day...


**"Ode to the Ironies of Spring"**

Day by day
Day after day
I do favor toil
Time, I do not waste
I bring out the dead...

A mask is a mask
Their faces
I do not see
A job is a job
I bring out the dead...

No places to give
fair respite for
their souls, hope
is the only essence, evermore
I bring out the dead...

Wondering next, who
shall it be? Me?
Oh the wickedness,
It never rests
I bring out the dead...

**"Plague"**

Even in the todays,
every time I step over a rain puddle
the reflection looking back up at me
always reminds me of my past.

How many other puddles, stepped
        in, on, over, through, around, before
yet they all look the same.
Always a gray, cloudy composition
        rarely ever colors, because
        most rain puddles do not fall
        on sun-shiny days
        just a gray, murky reflection, always.

And if one were to fall into
through to
the other side of the puddle,
what direction would one's life
have taken differently?

Always walking forward
        because one never walks backward
        through rainstorms
but a reflection of an opposite direction, per chance?

Not quite a shadow, nor a mirror
but re-seeing yourself again
and passing infrequently as the weather allows,
checking in on the other,
always passing and watching
the years grow older,
never speaking or even a nod,
just an acknowledgement
that even through all the rains,
your other self is still there.

You know you've thought about it...

**"Self-reflections in rain puddles"**

Your aura
entered the room
before you did

      announcing
      I've found you again

signaling
a change in my life
as I knew it
      (what a change it was)

and another lost
soul journey
begins again,
again.

The essence of time
behind leaves its ashes.
Memories burned,
lying charred and scorched
along this ceaseless path
of life, the winds
molding and shaping
a new change, another
chance at another life,
gambling once more
to get it right,
this time.

In a century of eons,
my travels
have been long
and my search
evermore, seeking
a commonality of souls
weary as mine own
and a final place to call home...
beside you.

**"The Attractions of a Wayfaring Soul Traveler"**

*'Reminessence'…*

The smell of a memory
the perfume of déjà vu
a waft of sadness, sorrow
always the same
always.

Baking bread
and chocolate chip cookies
will sell houses,
but what barters our psyches
to the human condition?

A distant field
this morning, mists
of the nighttime, rising
to greet another day.
The summer warmth
proofing a meandering fog,
low-lying
but just the same.
Just as my memories of you
always the same
always.


**"Fog on the fields, reminiscent…hazily"**

Ascension is never cheap;
at what price does the soul
profer another golden coin?

Seeking a higher ground
always begs forgiveness
          of one's immortal morals
          of one's mortal debts.

For what cost
does one realize
there are no concessions,
no allowances to be redeemed,
when acquiring elevation?

Gambling with one's psyche
as a psychic ante in the game of life,
the house knows no edge.


**"Ascension, be careful what you wish for…"**

The opening chime of my hearing aids
begins another day.

In the stock market of my mind
I can only wish my future shares
         HOPE, up -- FEAR, down
hold no average between the two.
There was no bell to ring,
no bell to hear.

Deafness reigns.

Stepping out in the world
        no birds awakening to early morning songs
        daffodils bloomless from late night storms
        trees limbs hitting the snooze button on Spring
        and yet the clouds still rumble, bemoaning the miles they
        must travel still.

Tranquility, once again.
Quietness reigns.

In the lonely distance,
a faint train
whistle, sounding
an early morning alarm
for those who know no time,
another day begins…

**"The Deafening of Silence"**

Our daily dailies
and routines,
dallying in circles
and keeping time,
never mind the repetitiveness.
Tomorrow is always another day.
And regardless of what's said,
it is always promised.
To someone.


The "drive-time" concept,
analogous to most any day
filled; excitement, frustration,
awkwardness, competitiveness;
contemplating always,
how did it get like this?


The traffic jam on an
old day planner padfolio page...
the breakdown lane no further over
than the bottle of pills or wine,
always kept close by
just as with any emergency flare
for those multi-carpool thoughts and pileups.


Tomorrow...always promised to someone.


**"Ouroboros-ian Commutes"**

Shaking the umbrella open and close
a thousand times, or so it seems...
every last raindrop clinging
to the badly over-stretched nylon
       one metallic rib poking through black fabric,
       a robotic arm gone astray, awry
       waiting to scratch anything at all


Upon opening the front door, a poorly tethered bell
attached by some frayed leather cord,
not quite chimes, but "tinkles" a welcome
to most any independent bookstore
in America


Slightly stomping wet boots on some
cheap plastic "Welcome" mat
       slightly...because it's always
       "Old Librarian Voice" hours
       inside the bookstore
I turn to glance out the plate-glass
window front, old-gold banker's lettering
announcing the store's name
in dyslexic reflection


Why,
in any big city
glancing out any plate-glass window
seeing the same gray pavement that's beyond drenched
under a dusk-lit monotone sky of musty orange-yellow saturated air,
why does this view always look the same?


**"Book Store"**

Souls, no longer
the keepers of mercy,
kindred spirits seeking warmth,
seeking solace from the misery
of long forgotten ages,
times when summer suns
no longer shone,
and memories drifted
expediently faster than
cloudless days.

Of yore,
autumn frosts bemoan
the coming of another dauntless moon,
another epoch of listless souls, wandering
seeking to gain enlightenment,
to find their noumena
once again.


**"Winter, darkest…"**

The beach house
        sunlight through the shades
        casting shadow-grates upon the floor
a mid-morning heat
rising outside from the apple-pie-warmth asphalt
creates shimmering day-ghosts taunting
to come outside, to brave
the coming heat of another day.


The shadow-grates remind
me...life in the city still
awaits – one must always return.
To what; the bustles and hustles
non-existent here? To faster
paces, everywhere to be
yet nowhere to go? To gray
days, ones that only
matter to a page-a-day desk calendar?


The day-ghosts are in repose
now, wrapped in cumulous shawls.
A breeze blows gently, rippling
the shadow-grates ever slightly,
a reminder they too have paces
to keep, the floor their
only canvas to traverse.


Again...a new day begins.


**"Beach House Blinds (shadow-grates)"**

**"Beach House Blinds (shadow-grates)"**
**Photo: Steven Wuebker**

**Inspiration for "Beach House Blinds (shadow-grates)"**

On a walk
I see fish
jumping in the pond.
Today,
several were doing a pas de deux.

The concentric ripples
growing ever outward, never fading
reminding me of
just how far
we have come,
just how much further
we have yet to go.

Concentric distancing
while nature may abhor its vacuums
it craves still…uniformity, conformity
in a social sort of way,
leading by example,
leaving behind its detritus-
it has no time to wait.

And I walk on…

**"Concentric Ripples"**

When you put the lid back
            on a glass candle jar
notice the flame burning still, brightly,
until it begins to realize
its own lack of oxygen.
A few short flickers at first,
dimly, then growing smaller
shorter
less strong.

A whisp of smoke begins
to unfurl from the ether within,
            a light "poof" if the jar
            were not soundproof
and the flame extinguishes
upon itself.

The smoke, racing itself towards
its own glass ceiling,
            clamoring as only smoke clouds do
            seeking an escape
            a breath of fresh air
            another wick to solace
heaves one final whisp,
only to fold back upon itself as well.

Yeah…kinda like life.


**"Life in a candle jar"**

It's not the leaves
themselves, but
the spaces between
the leaves,
that is what we should notice…

I see you, crescendoing
beyond the trees,
full as the day
is bright,
a veil of midnight clouds
allowing a glimpse
but always concealing
if nothing else,
a few lunar rays.

Come, part the clouds!
Shine upon night, brighter!
Darkness but a faint memory,
Silhouetted - you appear.

There'll be no sleep
for the waves
tonight.


**"Full moonlight through the trees, high"**

Two corporate pricks
        (yeah I used to be one)
standing in line at the local
coffee bar, "see and be seen" scene
no cares in the world
        other than the graphs
        better be on an upward swing
profits, sales, forecasts, ROIs,
and income equals greed.

        (Mask? What mask?)

Standing tall, standing aloud
"look at me! invincible,
as I should be!"
        If trees were people,
        the redwood forests
        stand no chance against some.
Tossing a handful of quarters
upon the counter, too busy
to make change, to busy
to make a change...
        "toe the line! out of step – no way!"

Holding a mid-morning meeting outside
in a rain shower does not make you...
        You probably learned social distancing
        long before the primates even learned to spell.

Everything's alike, perfectly
aligned, in the forest of your mind.
The daily grind, coffee and more,
still one of us,
you are still one of us...


**"The Regimentation of a Pine Forest"**
(ruminations on a corporate scene)

Dawakening
Dawn awakening

Meanwhile, dusk fighting
for the covers of night,
holding onto one last
glimmer of moonlight
before relinquishing
another day to begin…

Nighttime sadness recedes
        just as the ocean tides
allowing fresh sands a new canvas,
another day on which to make its mark.
Nature's memories are brief,
only a wave away
from eternal nothingness…

**"Dawakening"**

Walking out into the morning
      the night's yawns subsiding
      while symphonic crickets pack away their bows
smelling memories as they flood the senses
like an acid flashback from days past.

The whippoorwill's moaning its morning
call to arms, welcoming the heat
of an already begun day.
Someone's cooking bacon over
an open campfire: smells
like this...one never forgets.

The lake gently laps its shores,
collecting the carcasses of nature's
last-night catch – a hint of fish decay
with a dash of pond kelp provides
a morning buffet for the early rising gulls.

The rays of Mother Sun
shining through her cloudy veil,
      offering an outreach of warmth
an eternal maternal embrace after
coming home from the late shift.

The trail is long, it heeds
to where I must go.
Shall I not get started?
The memories will remain
upon my return, welcoming once again...


**"Mornings at the lake"**

alcoholics build mansions
out of ice cubes

maraschino cherries
being the chimney caps
or weathervanes

all depending on what color
the booze is that night...

hopes, dreams, mortar, bricks
all washed away
in one great flood,
one great blackout,
one great human disaster

one for the road, babe
one for the babe, road
one more...
one for...
hell, gimme another round...

**"Another Round"**

Some any bedroom, America…

Tacked on a wall, a posterboard-size
black velvet Thin Lizzy poster,
a black light in a fluorescent tube
shorter than the industrial white ones
found in any high school cafeteria,
shining upwards, unguarded against
any spills or falls or breakage,
its purple glow casting about…soothing.


A half-assed attempt at macrame
hanging in the corner, a false
project for home-ec if there ever was one.
Three brown wooden beads and one orange
        just to stand out
        to be different from others
        no matter the size of the crowd
decorate the rope work,
and an ass of a half-tassel hangs loosely,
decorating the bottom of the rope monstrosity.

What used to be plush-quality shag carpet
strands
oranges and browns
once-yellows
a solitary green
tossed randomly and island-ish,
hiding stains and secrets well.
Always has…always will.


The super-single waterbed
        "baffles are for pussies."
        the salesclerk said
taking up the entire room,
an ocean liner drydocked
in mid-suburbia, waves included
on the inside. Set sail!

(continued)

A little black stash bag
hidden somewhere amongst, tucked somewhere;
under a siderail of the bed
maybe behind a dresser
or the furthest reach in a dark closet
everyone has one. C'mon!


Rolling papers. Lighter – a Zippo if you're lucky.
Wrinkled plastic sandwich baggie
        invented when sandwiches used to be a dime
now just a dime-bag,
always short a few "pennies"
but it's the price we pay.


An old aquarium tank
sitting still in another corner,
never having left the black metal stand
I guess it calls its "eternal home".
I'm not moving it.
I'll get a lizard someday.


One final hit, my doobie
has smoked itself into a roach.
        (oh the creativity of being high!)
Tamping out the last ember into my marble ashtray
I exhale into dreamland.
I see this every night,
hoping I'll remember it some day
        long in the future…
hoping they play Thin Lizzy in heaven.….

**"Channeling my inner teenager self – 1970s"**

After having chased you
        for a century of eternities,
I know in my heart's soul
we have shared past lifetimes,
        a partnership of some form.


Having found you
        somehow
        again
in this life,
I'll be damned
        if you think
you'll slip away
        again
        somehow
on an easy path.


The veil is thin, my friend.
You only get to glimpse
        (never part, ever)
the sheerness of what you see,
however shimmery and enticing
maybe…it may be.


Aeons and centuries await,
and I have nothing but time.
        (time, but nothing)
There's past lives to make up for
and future lives to attain to…
but we still have to live this one.

For the path is not a race,
because the journey never ends…


**"Prometheus the Forethinker rides solo again."**

"Skating on a thin putting green
like a frat boy during Hell Week
-fearless of his own fearlessness-
hoping a "peace pipe" full of weed provides
a greater chance at "success salvation"
than standing around
with a bible in his hands,
praying ironically, to some
figment of his own imagination,
always wondering…
how the fuck did I get here
and when do I wake up from this dream?"

*Damn…I need more coffee.*
*Those mid-day stress breaks*
*are killing me.*

## "Skating on a thin putting green"

Marge is on her third martini
Ken is on twice as many beers
Blanche has a plateful of canapes
　　　it's that kind of party, one with airs

George has dropped a cigarette
Bill is opening even more wine
Sally is bitching about eggnog
　　　it's that kind of party, no one cares

Elaine has a Santa brooch
Louise found a new job
Sam just double-dipped, again
　　　it's that kind of party, everyone stares

Donald smells of old scotch
Marilyn is feeling her cramps
Dorothy forgot her daily meds
　　　it's that kind of party, anyone's affair

And me,
I put on an air of caring while staring at all the affairs…

# "Ahhhhhhhhhnother Holiday Party"

"Tophat o' the evn'g to ya...
beyond this gate
lie stairs, await.
Won't you join me,
why don't cha?

Me walking stick
but a prop, proper
accessory for journeys ahead.
Still, why not join me
for a night of never-end?

Traverse beyond, at a
cemetery gait – souls a'rest
and shall not awake.
Darkness of the moon, by
we shall be lead...
won't you join me, still?

Turrets of fear, fear not...
doorways beyond, scarier much...,
Yes, not all souls slumber, come...
for tonight, together, we toil...
so glad you joined me."


**"Mr. Straw, vespillō"**

**"The Night Traveler"**
**Photo: Kevin Buntin**

**Inspiration for "Mr. Straw, vespillō"**

"Spend" me all your money
the yacht won't buy itself
pay for prayers to be sent
there's a bible in your TV

Send...to lead me not out of
temptation, but onward soldiers,
disguised as the christian
you want me to be

American steeples draped
in the flag, the tv said it so,
"bathed in the blood of jesus"
if only holier, you could see

There's a multitude of beatitudes
and gratitudes, platitudes
with attitudes, dude...
yes, there's a bible in your TV.

**"Tele-evangeli-vision"**

You know you've heard it before,
another lone train horn blowing across the horizon...

And I flashback
to how I got here
somewhere I'm not sure
I'm even supposed to be.

("Wake up. It's time. Let's get moving again.")

I've traveled
        deserts without names
        plains of molten asphalt
        nights by overwhelming beacons
        always at night, always
a long ways
a lot.

In packs, yet alone...
alone, yet not isolated...
another footfall in the night
is never afar, even though
my destiny is.

Papers? Documentation? What...?
Is this such a time for
unnecessary accoutrements?
Such as records? Identification?

A next meal. Water.
Unsoiled clothing not
cleansed from a stream.
My dreams becoming tangible,
my physicality anything but asleep,
these are the accessories
for what drives me
through all the nights.

(continued)

And I remember…
yes, I have traveled.
Settled now. Maybe?
A lot, and afar,
still beckon somedays.


**Remembering…while packing for a long trip."**
(immigration lamentation)

A lone country road
anywhere
like every other one
somewhere.

The metallic nose from
freshly tilled soil,
a weary farmer making
his morning passes across
an endless landscape of hope,
that future growth returns, again.

Winter's last grasp of January
remains, a semi-frozen tundra and
frost nothing more than dead weight,
holding down remnants
of overlooked weeds
while the morning chill wraps
itself around sunbeams,
relentlessly penetrating
and reminding

After a cautious nod,
I round the bend…


**"Awaiting Spring, too early"**

I drive through the projects
 just before dawn
 sunrise still an idea away
Random windows spread near nor far
 it doesn't really matter
 in the projects, nothing matters
Bedroom lights decorate the darkness
 a beacon for a third-shift worker
 a third tryst after last call for someone else
I've seen them both.

I wonder what their stories are
 random fodder for morning poets
 as another day of drudgeries begins
Wondering how many clones of the insides exist
 knowing I've probably seen them all
 insides and outsides, every story has them
Wondering how far I've come so far
 downward, upward – the spiral's always moving
 memories become tidal waves of tsunamis
I wonder why I still return.

**"Projects: Memory Drive"**

Waiting to burn
        just as last autumn's
        pile of detritus
                logs, twigs, timber,
                debris, branches
        all hardwood and
        meant to last a lifetime
        like
the memories of you.

A cold morning field
        the sun's rays trying,
        deciding, whether
        to start the day
                hiding behind
                last night's clouds
        even those seem to hang
        for a lifetime
        like
the memories of you.

How many times before,
        and here once again
flint and stone
in hand, even ashes
last a lifetime.
If you let them.

I strike the match…


**"Waiting to burn"**

What if American Indians
        built the Great Pyramid of Giza?
You know,
maybe as a beacon
to their once former, "forever" home?
A way back
to finding their way back
because somehow they knew, somehow,
they would once again be forced
from another homeland...
        best to ask here,
        is there ever a permanent "home"?

Solstices aligned upon eclipses,
guiding lights
        not always by nightfall
        not always by sky
shining to be the path
this time chosen, not for a future,
but for the journey itself.

There is a lot of sand in an hourglass
        an amuse bouche of time
        before the buffet of journeys commences.

...but for the journey itself...


**"What if...?"**

Silent as the dawn,
she watches.

Mother Nature's sirens
one by one
holding court against
      an unforeseen enemy
      an invisible enemy
while offering hope of
a better day to come…

Fear Not!
Spring has unveiled
its equinox,
allowing greenery
to subtly contrast
against winter's drabness…
Hope Yes!

Hope Yes!
among the ongoing ephemcrality
of fear…
Hope Yes!
against the rising tides
of hopelessness…
Hope Yes!

## "The Blue Beacon of Hope"

**"Huli Iksiks"**
**Photo: David Hellard**

**Inspiration for "The Blue Beacon of Hope"**

Mountains sometimes
　　　become fields
while fields always
become mountains
　　　if time is ever enough…


Rounding the trail
　　　out of the woods
　　　and through the clearing
the horse pauses
then meanders onto a field
of yellow mustard
　　　all waves, no grain
its ochre undulates.
Beckoning? Mimicking?


And in fields beyond
as manicured rows
of fully matured corn tassels
　　　pre-vacuum packed…
　　　nature abhors…
　　　what?
create waves of CGI-perfect
graphs, even more rows
undulating topographically
with and against the wind,
I wonder…
how soon till harvest?


**"An afternoon cantering gait taken beside
a cornfield on a summer day"**

Try describing art to a deaf person
and then tell me creative writing
          especially poetry
isn't an "artform" of art.


The key word being "creative"…
you can't just stop
at any Big Box store
and pick a poem off the shelf.


Well, you can
but it most likely will be
overlayed upon a bad lithograph
of kittens or a country waterfall.
          Throw in some apples and a flag = success!
          You are now several levels above
          garage sales and flea markets.
You'll rarely find poetry on a clearance rack-
believe me, I've looked.


So there is beauty in the written word.
          "Eye of the beholder"
One of the key words (again)
in that phrase is not "of".
But you already know that.
You read it…


**"Art, 2"**

Three crows in a field
unbeknownst to them
     the first seasonal frost
     has come and gone
     so many times already
pecking away at a semi-frozen buffet
of random corn kernels dropped
by some anonymous farmer's combine
on one of its many pass-overs,
     trying to score one extra cent
     trying to score one extra kernel
          it's all profit before winter finally settles in
          for both parties involved.

Winter is coming
     slower than the tree sap already concentrating itself
fast and hard though, when it arrives.
It always does.
It always is…


**"Winter again…..again."**

The slow
constant
monolithic
clicking
melody
of the wheels
      the same on this train
      just as any other train
      always
reminding me of journeys past
bringing me to you
taking me away from you
      the same as this journey
      just as any other journey
      always.

The smell of spent grease
still warm from friction
permeates the railcar
flash-mobbing my memories
of past Christmas mornings spent
inhaling the fake "smoke" fumes
from the electric engine
of my childhood train set
while it circled
around and around
the shiny tin tracks
powered by
a hot metal box
that would shock you without warning.
      Always.

The whistle blows,
a horn yawns,
the wheels continue,
clicking and rolling along,
only slower now
      the same as my memories of you
      just as any other memory
      always.

**"The last 20 minutes on the train into
L'Enfant Plaza, Washington DC"**

Some shit-stained
                        bathroom
some shit-stained
                        Highway 57-368-9-753fuckIdon'tknow
the air, freshener
trying, shit-stained
                        as well.

Junkies' spent tools
lying in the corners-
syringes, or what's left
after the glass shatters,
pointing towards the
commode base
                        shit-stained.

The tiles used to be pale
                        almost lime green
                        but not quite
now cast in gray
                        subway tiles
that will never see
a train out of here.
                        Ever.


**"a place you'd never tell anyone you've ever been…"**

From my point of view
          perspective
          wherever somewhere is
the mountain appears
through the clouds,
both shaded masses of black and white.


Autumnal forestry hues
          already taken their cue
have long since fallen
to the ground,
leaving an opposing pallet
          gray and clear
for the mind's eye to process.


The haze, lingering
from another day's fraught,
provides a barely-sheer covering
as Mother Earth dawns
her evening gown,
giving a paparazzi's glimpse
          (flesh caught in a flashbulb)
of another day winding down…


**"Hard Dusk"**

The "not quite summer, yet..." rainstorms
leaving their smell of wet cement
          like wet dog, one always knows
hanging in the air,
so far away from becoming
a "fresh linen" scent;
the metallic-ness of it all will linger.


Windows open, slightly breezy days
that require no a/c. Dampness.


We all wish summer would
arrive just a little faster, even though
we'll all bitch about the heat
before the 4th of July.


Wondering if the memories
of summers-past
will return to their fruition before
the first stone fruit of the season arrives...
seeds of hope planted
as the last sunset of Labor Day pools
recedes into bays of hope,
trying desperately to hang on to
and remember that smell of chlorine
because it's vaguely reminiscent
of springtime storms.


**"Early storms"**

Definitely not nearly everyone
        but some people have
        a most succinct dark side.

From where, it does not matter.
It just matters.

Could be one of the seven sins…

pride
greed
lust
envy
gluttony
wrath
sloth

deadly, enticingly
pleasurably, definitely

or something like that.

One always keeps it in check
        just as the many secrets
        only a carnival barker knows
but it lingers…it's always there.
Succinctly.
Definitely.


**"Dark Matters (from whence)"**

Maybe memories are in vain,
not meant to be remembered...
just ghosts haunting our pasts, lingering.

A faintly glimpse of what used to be
          wandering, wondering, wishing, hoping – all of these
only to be carried away on a rain puddle stream
and always replaced by a barren drought
that never seems quiet quenched.

Yeah, maybe memories are in vain...


**"Early Morning"**

When you look in the bathroom mirror
       you see a reflection.
       Opposites, but a reflection, nonetheless.
       Your left becomes right, and versa-vice.
       An opposite.

But your eyes still remain the same color.
Your hair stays the same shade, ginger-red or summer-bleached.
The shirt you are wearing remains the same, stripes still striping whichever way.
The wallpaper behind you stays the same, reflecting a bad olive-green shade still.
The doorway leading into the bedroom, pauses long enough to show some carpet.
The queen-sized bed with the late 80s maroon/green faux-marble comforter; the same.
The digital clock on the nightstand, reading 11:11, the am/pm light long burned out. Same.
The shade-less window, beaming out into the side yard…the colors of Spring. The same.

So even while everything is reflected as its opposite, it's still the same.

So then, what is a reflection of time?
       The amount of seconds it took you to read the above lines?
       The length of each sentence?
       The pondering of going back to read them again?
       There is no hidden meaning.

And opposites, do they really attract?
Do mirror-opposites attract each other…colors and stripes be damned?

For future reference,
maybe there is a hidden meaning…

*"what is the opposite of time?"*

**"Opposite of Time"**

I have dreams
        nighttime ones
        daytime ones
        ones of achievement, ones of deceivement.
        I have dreams.

Time has slowed, for some reason.
        Winds of tar
        keeping my dreams
        in oozes, in places
        on no map that
        will ever include La Brea.
        Time has slowed.

Yet, the sun makes haste
across the kitchen tiles
and countertops
with a purpose
and the audacity to be anywhere
else
today.

I have dreams.


**"Winds of Tar"**

My circus beckons...
(will you answer its call?)


Least you not be judged,
then judge me not, as well.
For I have travelled...oh yes.
Far and wide and everywhere
**NOT** in between...


So judge?
A supreme misunderstanding
on your part, I dare say.
Your soul is anything but
a three-ring circus, as well.


My spots and tatters
have brazened the rains of many hells,
        my hat, an esoteric gift from a
        Venice Beach thrift shop for souls;
        the hip ones will jump any train
        bound for a further nowhere, any day.
        Every day.
You're here, aren't you?


The autumnal spoilage
        because what else does one call
        rotting leaves? Beauty?
camouflaged the journey of your dreams,
your nightmares, your life.


But mostly...your nightmares.


You are here now, no "where" but everywhere.

(continued)


What's that you say:
       "But I don't have a ticket!"
Silly, you little silly…
not every journey requires a cost,
but every cost requires a journey.


Come!
Deboard!
"TreeStation" is not your destination;
for my rails never end in eternity.


There are many more hells left,
more fire-proof souls to extinguish,
more…many more to bring to the circuses.


The clown has finally been sent in…


**"Il Pagliaccio Della Morté (the clown of death)"**

**"Il Pagliaccio Della Morte"**
**Photo: Kevin Buntin**

**Inspiration for "Il Pagliaccio Della Morté (the clown of death)"**

If my love were a peony
its fragrance would be of a rose,
because sometimes love,
love is just like that.

If my love were a rose
it would often remind me of spring,
lilacs always arriving late
to the daffodil's party.

If my love were a daffodil
its tuxedo-stance would always beckon,
stoutness becoming
through the cold, winter mornings.

For my love has always been of a garden
not always a secret place
but always kept near
close, and once again as
petals pressed between wax paper...


**"tres hermanas"**

*Lesson 1*
  "Because...Hey-Sue's!"
did you hear the good news?
the children are taught
at a young age,
always respect your elders.
no one ever says how elderly,
antiquated, how artifacted
  ("there's one for the antiquities!")
the intended target of respect must be.
just believe it, daily and frequently,
  "Because...Hey-Sue's!"

*Lesson 2*
  "Because...Hey-Suze!"
did you read the good word?
there are a lot of them
out there, just not
all looking up, out, and/or further,
the inward words are frowned upon,
looked down upon; they mean nothing
  ("there's one for the confessional!")
if the end is never justified by some random mean.
just believe it, daily and frequently,
  "Because...Hey-Suze!"


**"And people wonder why religion as a
second language is so hard to learn..."**

The shelves are barren-er
        than they used to be
at any big-box-give-a-customer-a-coupon
"Make sure they leave happy!"
retailer.
Emptier.

But they have been before...too.
Everything is cyclical-
        bicycles, icicles, epicycles, sickles
winter wheat, anyone?
"This too shall pass..."
seems to be heard a lot sooner
these days.
Cyclical.

Everything is just "Inflation and a Winter War" perfect!
Now what "what now?" is next?

Empty cycles...once again.


**"Inflation and a Winter War"**

As Mother Nature's polar bear beard
of a frost settles upon the windowsills
        drafts on the panes
        sometimes an only friend
I'm reminded just how many sunrises
remain until Groundhog's Day.
And I'm reminded
does it ever really ring true?
Forecasts...the projections?
The scope of horror our horoscopes sometimes bring
compares nothing to the often-times tragic length of waiting winter out.

        The blueness of navy mixing in with the sky's nighttime black
        and yet darkness is still not perfectly clear,
        cloudless skies only mean some other planet
        somewhere, is sharing a starless night.

There will be no "red sky at night" warnings
this time of year. Sailors will take delight still.

The drafts continue to shed Mother Nature's dandruff
        tossing a final log onto the night's fire
        only seems to attract more to the flames
winter moths will be my company this evening
deftly greeting me soon enough with one less sunrise to await.


**"The carnival barker in winter"**

*"Goddammit lady, quit honking!*
*I have to pay my fucking bill*
*just like you do...!!!"*
I think to myself, mirror-glancing
past the back-seated twins,
locking eyes with the driver
behind me. She flips the bird.
I look away.

I wonder what time Paul will be home,
this time, bragging about dragging us
to some other basement football party
this weekend. "MOM!", The twins start to shout.
"Kelvyn and Ashleyee, stop it!" bursts forth
a little too loudly, to forcefully. Said, not thought.
Silence ensues. The line moves forward.

Did I mix up that tax bill
with the cookie order form?
My wallet has slipped between the seats
and my bag has a new scuff, stain, both.
My platinum card is my warrior shield
in battles for greater kingdoms than this,
a drive-thru line at rush hour.

As I casually extend my middle finger
out the window, directed at all and none,
I pull out of line, away, wondering
did I buy enough wine?


## "An exasperated mess in Suburban, America"

A solitary drop
of dew
clinging for warmth
to a lone blade of grass,
basking in the morning's sun
before loosening its grasp,
allowing the coldness of spring
once again…

Midnight frost
on the windowpanes,
not quite the canvas
covered, yet reminding us
the dog days of summer
are still a want of yore...

The flowering moon
departs slowly, not
yet ready to make haste
for pastures beyond its horizon,
reminding us, like memories,
our nights are forever long
sometimes forever cold...


**"Winter, never ending"**

Cresting the ridge
at sunrise,
the spring morning
greets me as if
I were born once again…

A galaxy's worth
of Jerusalem Stars
cover the mountains I must tread,
there will be no snow this time
baring my path once again…

The river winds
and turns, shallow
but not innocent,
it keeps silent company
a fickle mistress once again…

The lonesome tree, pointing
a broken weathervane
to my Star of David,
its barren branches, barc
bare as my soul once again…

And I ride on, once again…

**"Untitled"**

**"Tiskay"**
**Photo: David Hellard**

**Inspiration for "Untitled"** (previous page)

$$a = c$$

because

$$a = b \text{ and } b = c$$

therefore

music = memories

food = memories

furthermore

food = music

and

memories = memories
except for when they don't.

As defenseless as a shaved porcupine in winter,
there's a reason cows get massages in Japan...

This must be a poem.
There's supposed to be lines like that in them.
Why?
Because.
But this is NOT middle-school English-Lit.
It doesn't have to make sense.


Remember that food and music stuff from earlier?
What kind of songs were you humming in the middle grades?
What food did you pick at during the cafeteria lunch period?
> - *everyone has sopped grease with cheap napkins from a rectangular "pizza"!*

There will always be songs, foods.
And thankfully if we are lucky,
there will always be memories...that equal something.


**"Abstractions and Memories"**

Adding thirds to a dinner party
always makes for more lively conversations...


When the ego met god
      for the first time?
      again?
      the last time?
          (does either really exist?)
I wonder how the conversation went.


*Was there an agenda?*
      a powerful slide or two,
      bullet-pointed topics
      to debate and refute?
      or
      a list of grievances and sins;
      each mortal, universal, and uniform
      in its respective nature, each offensive.


Were there excellent spreadsheets
graphing
each
existential
question?


Why not invite the twins,
      numen and psyche
seat them next to each other
and ruminate a topic?


Debates can rage for days,
even the ones we have within ourselves...


**"When Ego met God"**

What's the going exchange rate these days
between karma and souls?


Does anyone still accept universal coins
or did they become like the Sacagawea Dollar?
        Fun. A novelty.
        Still given as gifts to grandchildren.
        Still heavy.


"Karma's a bitch!" – ever met karma?
Anyone?


Does karma ever really catch up to us?
To itself?
Living now to ensure your karma
for when...the future?
Your next reincarnation?


And really...
are we earning karma or spending it?
Eternal deposits into the karma account
and some souls, still overdrawn.
Why not just live within your means?


We all take loans against karma
        knowingly kiting our souls
        between numerous actions
        daily, overdrafts be damned.


And at the close of the mortal business day,
all that really matters
is that the books are balanced.


**"The Currencies of Being"**

The intertwined bands of the universe
(circumferences diagonally as well)
lock timelessness in its place,
sometimes pausing long enough
to catch a glimpse
of a simple lifetime
suspended for the memories
to almost catch up – "déjà vu"
they like to call it.

Connections made,
(and forever knowing, again)
time after time and again,
always getting disconnected
from the eternal group chat
at the most inappropriate times – "premonition"
they like to call it.

But ponder not that, for life
(banding upon itself, once again)
always reminds us there were previous bands,
different universes that encircle the ones
we only believe in our dreams,
the connectivity...that shimmeriness
one always sees on black ice,
but only with their mind's eye...
right when it's too late – "well, you're screwed."
they like to call it.

**"The intertwined bands of the universe"**

And we wintereth on...

The nuclear clock nothing but anymore,
　　　a scrambled mess of alarms
　　　and a secondhand askew,
　　　telling time no longer
　　　telling us our time may be shorter still.

The media
a mass of everything amiss
　　　bombs, traffic reports,
　　　weather, back to bombs
　　　because the traffic sucks
hanging onto that secondhand
stronger than a trapeze artist's

　　　　　last grip, last grasp

because if it fails, if it falls
　　　a media amiss among the masses
　　　pays no electric bills.
War sells...even on credit.

And we wintereth on...


**"Climbing icicles and chasing snowbows"**

Sometimes…even artists get the blues
        (ah! another irony of life!)
taking up their instruments
returning to their "safe space"
        a common breakroom of the mind
channeling their intuitions
        just as they always have
        so many times before
        again
seeking solace via whatever canvas
presents itself that day;
it never matters really.
The mental yoga will always
find itself a mat; downward dog, be damned!


The muse is only human
        and the full moon rises tides
        a faction of the imagination
        maybe?
sharing its *bipolar-ness*
across many spectrums
        good days, bad days
        but there are always days.


Self-medication is the best relief
        a double-dose of creativity
        may cause side effects
        such as relief and a rapid heart rate
Use with caution.
May be habit-forming.
Never titrate the muse…
overdoses are preferred.

(continued)


In the end
          (ah! is it ever really finished?)
the canvas is covered
the artist is exhausted
the muse is reposed
and a single                              word
                          line-
                    brushstroke
          comma,
        drip
appears
causing armies of azures, lazulines, and sapphires
to amass for the following day's battles
          no matter how pale or faded or tired
because the symptoms are always there...

Break time is over. Clear the room.


**"a mild case of the ceruleans"**

the wicked spear of the path
a broken lamplight, shadows not cast
skulls of gnomes roaming gardens no more
darkness is not my tale, it's
only the beginning of the light…

a quiver of twigs brings no fire
my shawl, not one of redemption
the barren fields of early summer
seen, far as the scarecrow flies
…would you like to hear my tale???

**"Untitled"**

**"This Way…"**
**Photo: Kevin Buntin**

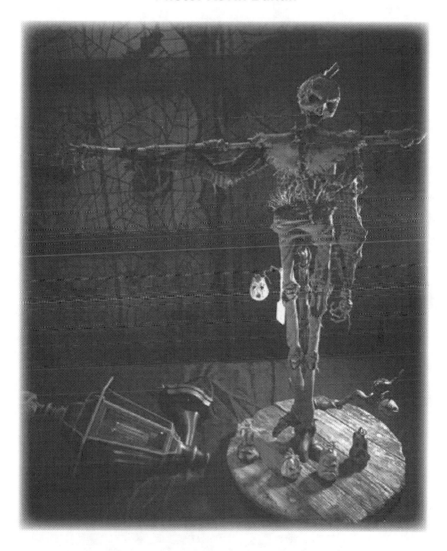

**Inspiration for "Untitled"** (previous page)

*"Dude, we're not middle-age...we're older than that." – says he.*

So says the dude
who sounds as if
the middle-ages
are yet to be seen.


**"Dude"** - Maybe a generation ago...
now just a case of sleep apnea
in place of the dreams and fantasies
            (fantasy-dreams)
of growing up a mid-1980s life.


Dreams...tucked away
into some dark corner-closet's corner,
        maybe in a box labeled
        "memories"
        and held together by duct tape
                full of wishes, remembrances,
                and that now too-small
                first concert t-shirt
                of the first concert ever!
Dreams...of a time ago, of a safe
place ago.


Ironic how times of high-anxiety
seem such a safe place
in the todays of today.


But just as with these flash-mob memories
you are recalling now,
this too is a slight digression...

(continued)

So aging.
Generations.
Come and go and always.


Bequeathing their resentments
of dreams interrupted and
fantasies that remain just that,
along with their box of "memories", tossed...
so long ago, even they cannot remember when.


Middle-aging...aging,
just growing older...
growing out of those old concert t-shirts,
growing into new memories of new pasts,
and wondering...what is it that
always makes us want to stay young for so long?


**"On middle-aging"**

There was a line once
something about
don't wake up hating the world...

They say you shouldn't "hate"
anything
that it will follow you through your life,
however many of them there may be.

Maybe that's also what they mean-
        "born again"
even evil must be born again
for it to continually exist
within the universal world.

So carrying it with you, hate.
Recycling unnecessary emotions
centuries over, of them all
hate always seems to find a way.

Yes, there are bounty hunters
of the soul, seekers
who strive to right the wrongs
of our past discretions,
however numerous they may be
however farther they may reach.

Sometimes we place the bounty
upon ourselves.
Yet one cannot awaken daily,
grudgingly holding eternal grudges
against never-righted wrongs.

Somehow, we all know deep inside
our beings, our world
isn't wired that way.


**"Reincarnating revenge, recycling hate"**

After all
the rushes
the hurries
and
the on-the-go's...

Life.

The hearse behind you
will never use its turn signal.


**"Slow Down"**

Descending...
through the stratification
of nighttime clouds,
a hanging mobile project for the amusement
of some god's, perchance.

Sprawl...
the stratification of
a different meaning,
the nighttime urbaness
reminds me of my childhood
Lite-Bright® toy; the stretch
of neighborhoods, lights across
the thin, black paper
       holes punched randomly
       outside the lines
different colored pegs
       all are missing some
mixed together, not always
following the suggested patterns.

Because...it's prettier that way.


**"Landing at night, Columbus, 3am"**

The gray, cloudy days of May...

The lion
a king of jungles
urban – suburban
makes no difference;
the plains are always the same
and that's too easy.

The lamb
a promise of peace
wartime – sleep
always a landscape;
there's always rain on the plains
and that's too easy.

The snake
a symbol of thievery
despair– heartbreak
all stolen just the same;
the plains' rains always reign
and that's too easy.

Society.
On a day-by-day,
"not always like this"
survival of the fittest
kind of day,
on some urban-landscapian sprawl
outside somewhere's inner city
where wartime is every day
on battleground sidewalks that never sleep.

Society.
Everyone plays a role,
spirit animals be damned.

The lion, the lamb, and the snake...
and the rain is the same on all the plains.

Society.


**"The lion, the lamb, and the snake"**

The Aurora Borealis.

Even if you don't believe
in some divinity of trinity,
or in some buddhist-leaning reincarnation,
or some traveling sideshow huckster
      with a trunk load of sweet elixir
see the lights just once.

One cannot look at those nighttime skies
and miss the concept of "universal" energy-
what else can it be?

If we even remotely question it,
all we are left with
is some random overhead projector
and a colorful, oil-filled petri dish
swarming all over some grail-like shroud
in some late-60s ballroom,
hoping for a miracle...
hoping to someday see the light...,

**"Aurora Borealis, credentis"**

Everyone needs a good harp-n-crie
every so often
>take that twisted *mental*
off the wall
rosin up that bow
>>("Live".....if you're hip.....if you're down........
maaaaaan!")
>and blast out a symphony
that will make the hills
want to be born again.

After a while, time, ego, age,...them all
>the twisted metal still hangs
upon the wall, but *mental* no more,
because even though the echoes
of long-forgotten concerts still ring,
the old songs just don't mean as much
anymore.


**"Harp-n-Crie"**

"ZAP!"
If you've had them, you know.
A permanent fixture residing in your daily life,
slowing waning as your false dependency
recedes a little more each day, but


"ZAP!"
out of nowhere-
that split nano-second of realignment,
        (a reset patch pushed through by the aliens?)
a slight 15-second hum afterwards,
leaves you wondering
how long till the next one?


"ZAP!"
Wishing they would stop but then
not caring because "donuts!"
and you know they taste good and you don't
care, and your jeans begin to care more
by clinging tighter, divorcing
themselves from your belt because
cookies and donuts, but you don't
care because of another low-maniac
thought stream that keeps you
company until the next 60mgs are due.
Oh, donuts!
"ZAP!"


**"Brain zaps; the anti-depressant alarm"**

I stand with my fiddle, attending
the spring flowers of May,
begotten from the April
showers of a dreary day

The daffodils and pansies
will come and grow,
and the dandelions will wither
in my garden so

Melodic birds, the cadence
of their morning songs,
awakening and keeping time
as the days grow long

This world too will pass, just
as I have traipsed
through my garden so,
always stop and smell
the roses, then listen
for the strings of my fiddle low

Another cloud, a ray of sun,
another shower, a sign
that life has begun,
from my morning perch
to the evening stoop,
unlike the leaves of winter,
may the memories of
my garden, never droop.

For my fiddle will always play…

## "The Girl on Top of the World"
For Jean, for Mike

**"The Girl on Top of the World"**
**Photo: Steven Wuebker**

**Inspiration for "The Girl on Top of the World"**

Why are most sounds
always so lonesome?

What is it about the universe...
that instead of feeling omnipotent,
      that shooting straight up off the Earth
      one can travel into forever...
      and then some beyond
what is it about the universe that makes us lonely?

      The multitude of dimensions
      unfathomable even in this lifetime
      create opportunities our mammal-ian souls
      are ever fearful of imagining.

Cast about in a universal ocean
and washing upon ethereal shores,
what's so fearful about that?

Yet, we are a lonely lot.

We cling, out of fear,
out of love, out of
fear of running out of love.

Solitude is becoming of us,
if we let it be.

The ironies of feeling lonely
while basking in solitude...
everyone does it.

We're not special.
We're lonely.

**"Lonely"**

A meandering stream
winding through banks lined
by an early-spring, daffodil-rush
of color
  the usual yellows
  greens and golds, variances
  in tone
all beauty just the same.


A wall of forest hugs
the valley, each watching
the other age through
Mother Nature's watchful gaze.


The log house, not quite
cottage and definitely
none of the trappings
to make a home...
has held court through
fewer storms; its kinship
with the forest, like the hardwoods,
only grows stronger and
weather ahead, be damned.


Spring in the valley
  (any age of anything)
and it always rings true
to be the same; scents
of post-rainstorm blooms
amid a hint of pine trees
and smoke from somewhere...
an early morning cocktail for the senses.
Mother Nature requires no "happy hour".

(continued)

The pastel watercolors of memory
will always linger.
It doesn't take much to transport
back to one's place...
remembrances are as easy
as talk is cheap.

Rose-colored pressed petals
will always fade...it's the book
they are pressed in
that makes all the difference.

Remember to walk that valley
from time to time.
The stream will always lead you back...


**"A valley in a field in springtime"**

Some people spend their lives behind bars
(liquids, places, metals, mental)
but what about those
who spend eternities behind pillars?
Our own defenses
          fortified stronger than any marble
often shield our mental castlements too well...
keeping out, keeping in;
is there a worse?

          We judge
          ourselves, others
          always have, always will.
          We judge.
          Because our pillars keep us safe
          or so we think.

Our daily existence,
always put on display
and always deserving "Best Actor"
awards, accolades, ribbons, and parades
even though there is only a jury box
reserved for one
in the pre-show, dinner-theater of our minds.

          Anxiety as an amuse bouche
          before the buffet of life commences?
          "Sure. I'll take several and Thank You."
          say a lot of people, now.

So, pillars.
Gateways, not so much.
Yet still, like any unknown
guest, virus, visitor...
we allow things to pass;
"through-only" is the intent.
If not, we judge.

(continued)

No bothers or worries looking for mirrors,
least not in these halls.
Long ago shattered, an escape attempt
not so much:
everyone knows,
even our reflections pass judgement.

Seeing ourselves, locked behind
mental pillars...

Eternally.

## "In the court of pillars"

*"A sponge of the world...I like that." – said she.*

What does one call
"aggressive osmosis"?
Passion? Drive? Ambition? Relentlessness?

Is it about absorbing and learning as much as one can about
anything?

Some spend days like a pale, pink
piece of fake cellulose,
holding court from the back
of the kitchen sink,
  one of a pack of four,
  one of a partial rainbow
long separated from the pack
to go on its own.

We step out into the world
on a daily basis, and
the evening news always bellows
"sensory overload" and "oversaturation"
but isn't this how we learn,
  an always unfolding roadmap
  that takes up half the front seat
  whenever traveling by car,
  knowing that once our destination
  arrives to us,
  that map will never
  be folded the same way again?
Yet we took the journey.

Sunlight never sees
the back ledge of that sink,
even though people still clamor,
beg even, on a daily basis
to be released from the shadows.

(continued)

Stepping that first step
into discovery, a new everything awaits;
that's the beauty of a sponge...
it can always be rung out
and it can always absorb more.

Be a sponge...but of the world.

## "Sponge"

My father, always excited
at the firewood find
of cedar logs. Downed
by natural chainsaws
or man's nature,
"seasoned enough" to burn,
to give off a blueish-purple
haze, a 1970s stoner's delight
floating in the smoke, never acrid
and never-quite-pine-enough,
yet a distinct scent
nonetheless.

Every time the family cedar chest
      of heirlooms, keepsakes, delicates, memorabilia
      (because some families are famous)
opens,
the same scent of pre-burnt logs
will always take you back to bonfires.
And no matter how many launders,
that not-quite-pine-scent always lingers,
the way old sweatshirts often times reek
in the mornings
after keeping a bonfire company the night before.


**"Cedar"** (for my father)

The serene calm
        almost an eerie weirdness
such as on some Christmas Eves, cloudy,
so much so, one would
be hard-pressed to believe moons exist...


When the temperature hangs
amongst a dampness, the air
not quite chilly enough to stay
outside long enough...but long enough
to warm up from the coldness inside...
some holidays are like that.


The calmness hangs, serene
and peacefulness compete,
the stillness pervades...
almost as if an hourglass of sand
pauses mid-downward-stream,
the world...for one's subjective moment...
hangs in the balance, not long enough
to do a complete reset, but long enough.
Just long enough.


Spring rains will emote the same
nostalgia...pausing long enough.
The same looking clouds, returning,
always leave us pondering moons...


Stillness.


**"Pondering Moons"**

The gray skies, daily.
Industrial revolution in reverse
seems to be amongst us these days.
Commonplace.


A war of threats is always raging
about the threats of war.
Nothing seems newsworthy anymore;
even that's breaking news to some.
Unfortunate?


The daily...gray skies.
Daily, the grind, day after day, again.
And again.
Daily.


And so we go on...and we make.
We make art.
We make plays and dances.
Their meanings float on everyday
dreams, everyone's nightmares.
Nocturnal has different definitions
depending upon its season.


The universal jumbotron of the mind
switched to the 2:53am snow-static
a long time ago...some people were too busy
adjusting the foil between their antennas
to notice.
And even that is breaking news to some...


**"Newsprint Poetry"**

Oh how our paths have crossed before...

It's the revolving debt we keep
with the universe
to be allowed the experience;
the duty of living.

This go-round, however brief,
your middle-classified life
in your middle-class mansion,
classified only by class and
the classlessness it ensures;
the duty of living.

Or the previous life of a fiefdom
warlord to the universe's stars, always
a forbidden king held high upon
thrones of metal only rhodium and palladium
can dream of being, overlording
to peasantry and misery, while
happiness escapes;
the duty of living.

Or that life's previous life, one
of lower than peasantry, a straw lean-to
only leaning against hope, a home awash
in an oatmeal-colored field
rarely seeing sunlight, meagerness
does nothing more to calm
the memories of previous kings;
the duty of living.

Oh before our paths cross again...
let us not be as kings in fields
or peerless peasantry within castles,
let us find one another quicker,
let our universal memories be clearer,
and may our karmic debt to one another
be some day paid.


**"While reincarnating memories..."**

# Postscript

"It's all about perspective..." – Steven Wuebker

*At the end of all the days, they are just words on pages...*

# Photo Credits

## Kevin Buntin

Kevin Buntin currently resides within the wilds of Troy, Ohio.

Art has always been a part of his life, literally. He doesn't do art out of pretense, or a desire for recognition or wealth - any artist can tell you what a waste of time that route to fame and fortune is! He does it because he always has; it is a compulsion, a need. If he stops, then he becomes ill.

The size of his work and the subject matter of it tend to focus on the microcosm rather than the macrocosm. They occupy the space left over in the world, the tiny places between the roots and the trees.

Books and stories have always been a large part of his life, along with music, and they have all walked hand-in-hand with his art.

His galleries and additional information can be viewed at @kevin_buntin on Instagram and Kevin E. Buntin on Facebook.

## David Hellard

David Hellard is a Portland-based photographer and digital artist.

His distinctive personal style has evolved from pure landscape and architectural photography into a fusion of photography, digital graphic design, and imagination in an effort to create works of art that evoke deeper spiritual and emotional responses.

His works can be viewed at www.davidhellard.com.

# Acknowledgements and Gratitude

Thank you to my husband Joel, for everything...your love, your encouragement and patience, your support, your "re-encouraging" to push the project through till its end, your understanding, your proofreading, and all the feedback...all of what it took to make this project happen! I love you "more" than words can say!

Thank you to my mother and sister for always supporting me in my writing endeavors from a very early age. Life's journey is well documented through our memories...my universal gift is writing about life and its memories. Thank you both for the love and support you have always shown!

Thank you David and Kevin for allowing me to share some of your art. A few of these writings were inspired by your works and lead to the first step in this book. Gentlemen, thank you both for being the artists you are...and for your friendship!

Thank you to my "beta readers"...a few wished not to be mentioned by name, so in respect and with fairness, I express my gratitude to each of you for your feedback, one and all. If you were one, you know who you are. Your insight was not taken lightly and was most helpful during this project.

Thank you to everyone at Balboa Press for their assistance and guidance while traversing the publication process of this book. It was an exciting journey... one worth taking that very first step.

And finally, thank you to the readers of this tome. You have given of your time and mental energy to peruse my words, hopefully finding some respite from your day. My gratitude will be forever appreciative and humble.

Thank you.

Printed in the United States
by Baker & Taylor Publisher Services